transfixion

bill lavender

New Orleans • 2009

GARRETT COUNTY PRESS

http://www.gcpress.com

Trembling
Pillow
PRESS

http://17poets.com

Acknowledgments

Gracious thanks to the following journals where
some of these poems first appeared:

Jubilat: "Coda for Federico García Lorca"
YAWP: "commander" and "salute"
Fell Swoop: "the game within" "event horizon"
Whatsanotherwordfor Press: "me" (broadside)
E•ratio: "ceremonial certainty"
fieralingue: "envoi," "one of a kind," "reply," "broken
rock," "rachel decides to get her eyes done,"
"ground"
Eleven Eleven: "agon," "bread"
Xconnect: "where after all" "ground"
Tata Nacho: "soon" "pastoral"
Prairie Schooner: "fair play" "nothing"

CONTENTS

transfixion

transfixion

for Dave Brinks

Hee… shal finde both an explicit contradiction, and a double transfixion, like that stroake of Phinees… pearcing with one speech through two at once.

Bishop William Barlow (1609)

The word "transfiction" has been coined to this interactive narrative system where users can interact with narrative machines (devices with computing power and containing databases of meaningful information).

Nandi Alok and Marichal Xavier (2006)

envoi

like birds singing
what we have
selves perched in the single soul

to see our cells as others see thus
unsettled stomachs
saying softly

non cessasti omnique
excruciare modo
to answer the chorus of cicadae

children getting into bed
then beginning to know
what damaged goods are

I know
this as a fever
or as you know love

upper arms resting
on the moon in your lap
stars sliding across

the city's
conflicting altitudes
rhythms of loneliness

little thoughts of seclusion
like a low trellis inside my head
son los dioses

I will go back for you
go fiddling in your suspicion
ghosts all round

everywhere in new bright parasols & waistcoats
breathing pear & quince
into old tomes

one of a kind

to give to see
to understand or think immediately
people's uses of smiling

ground of imago is fear
a paranoid metropolis
mouth & insides breathing

the one & only rift
green altar devious priest
sublimated afresh to sting down deep

my clay is hangman
our world stupor
opaque but silver

before a t-square of light
right through the body
waters & vegetation sprout

who carried off orithyia from the banks of
literature? her eyes
bent to the hours

she started talking to any & every
one watching the language
it's none of my business said the table

but the map we feel
a kind of love or plaything
trembling in sacred rites

reply

for Joseph Makkos

I know you I guess
about as well as I know myself
about as well as a summer night
or sculptured marble
tonal systems
languages like wolof
assume that sexes and shapes
rise among us in blunt reproach
beauty without strength
like the pools that stand in drains,
like the smudging mayflies
so june can have
her dwelling in the setting sun
her weathered plumage
it was america
satchitananda
yelling and shrieking
no leaves
no narrow views
to things below
island of the blowing wood
island of silver parapets
how we come to understand things
after tea and after the bridge
a palace on the water
& then to retrace your steps
at least the thing broke out
of all the goods I ever cared about
of a life sought
& a little bird our tinker and smith
you can lie back now

& mouth into the veins
of my earliest & happiest memories
of my life overseas
of the dark beneath & the bright above
of church & the state
but you will not have many
to choose from
child of this country
your rose is bold
as a basket along the banks
but have you ever loved
the body with a capital b
felt the calm returning
a desire to cry
to see the souls retiring
snatching chatter
through the shifts
a flash &
circling rivers
circling breath
& a circling
bitch still unresolved
wherever whyever
whoever you appear
alone before me
better to taste this frost
shrivelled by war
as the body perceives
its pitcher of honey
the same intention
the same splendor
the same furniture

the same wondering
about all that speech
the specific contour
the downward shift
that other people die
where trumpets chorus
memory is this place
experience and police
the voice
articulation
whether friendship or pleasure
be the motive
my love is the slow offense
not the mire of human veins
nor the fiction of wakefulness
but as red as ripe as could be this
bitter fruit

broken rock

station of the medium
heave of water like the
hand that whirls water

this which was so constant
without any need to be so
the gift which
all my life I tend

harp of shadows where I taste
my last & only flight

was it an unborn
doing the bridal stirrups
poor facts that burn

a feast of discourse & the
change that change awakens

rachel decides to get her eyes done

she opened her fen
& roads overgrew
flow of clichés over plateaus

examine these limbs
so cunning with tendons
opening & shutting

what does it matter if
no thin men of haddam
bring honeycombs dripping

plunder & absence
or sun & moon evade
light of understanding

dig these participants
to make the spirit groan
iconic points

of light you see
react to particles
to the cracking

to the shifts in your toyshop heart
what was he
that rivers run with falls

some hermit
in his cave
by his fire

up the highway his
widow regarded me like
an innocent fidgeting zebra

sea-girls reading
products of our time they
cower under the sea-pine

I will die on a rainy day
& stand here & hear
them wandering homeless

a sensual & timorous beauty
the steep ancestral brooking
I long to make

language is not for humans
not as they're born anyway
it helps to found

a sound of music
or brittle fig trees
what was & will be

leaf or vine
the flesh of laborers
inductive proof

the scarp she's thinking is going to turn
through imperialism's face
into oil & color

insisting a story lay
crouched in my head
chanting how the light may hap

under a plane-tree
with crowns & wreaths
what did nature give us

indians but english
& a stack of country corpses
our kin within

a railroad set out to
bring each of us home
& the war was subsumed in it

ground

I feel the worms ease through
this lonely house
& know its whole weight
above round gray stones

but the river is my friend
feel it laugh in your laugh
unable to control yourself
your imagination

dust-colored chandeliers
my mourning coat my chin
my sounds which raise me
my ways of keeping flame

should I begin again
by changing the story
the regular annual ring
faces pocked & patched

better to be vain than vainly
hope for standards
we natives of a place which knows
no limit

rock-chasms & loose stones
staring straight ahead to where
a witless movie genre or mystical
beat purples

disgraced already you suppose
a planetary futures market
a burnt sprig of rock-flower
a deck with goddesses & glitter

your love is lust your friendship cheats
each language pouring its vain
how you know who will come
through centuries

non si densior aridis aristis
sit nostrae seges osculationis
lovers who are free not
under any compulsion
to remember their french their czech
the catastrophic histories buried in each

little town these streets forever
long and lazy as a seal

our charges for & against
to be a great writer
to be like napoleon
to take from
vagrant dwellers in the woods
what you will not let me speak

children afraid of night
wrest behind the wall
exchange messages
obstinate & susceptible
zero's secret
surrounded by snakeskins

satellites scan surfaces
language can almost describe
flowers & weeds
crudely smeared life that
fed us tenderly
as stone against sky
as dew drips off the low branches
unnoticed into the stream

and when war-time came
a concrete river
wondered to what
or to whom to return

whatever roads
lie within
I want to know
this moment
singing & hungry

voices turning
logos stemming
smoking lamp light
where sirens abide
space grasped during ecstasy

a monster more complicated &
swollen with passion than any serpent
will wax & then dwindle
& it will make you laugh in spite of
the customary entreaties

a place with its own
trimmed rose
with its own pain
its own singing I

you hear the grating roar
the great robot preserve
unhonored unnoticed all this worth

and the empty branches
where our blood dries

the game within

when I die
or scythe it all

the mind we share
will still go on a

shrimp boat drunk
to bear witness

set the head & divvy the hair
bald spot in the middle of my chair

victims directly linkable to a chain
selling burgers & tacos

no way out of spiritual bog
but to consecrate the blog

why innocents in prisons
why the neighs of battle

where is abundance
where the pills that kept me going

I saw you painting
I saw a river unaffected by tides

I saw the image re-enter
as I see my soul reflected

in the crime-chalked sidewalk
in the sophic strewn voices

cave eye corrupting my darkness
working midnight's small thoughts

here in the spreading tree democracy's altar
do you hear would you listen

face up he rolls
a wide-open fall
where nothing exists but
the time of year

letting go of branches
tugging at the way
like a river that hurls
toward unremembered pleasures

he recognized the valley
at peace in nature & language
his sangfroid self a frond
returned to a high strand

man– what a feeble tenant
what part of yourself can't be
hauled in a shroud
or voices can't worm through

poplars stand still as death
like a turn or gesture
a headdress of fresh flowers
or a story without plot

a river sings
even at dark
even on the ocean floor of taboo
even out of mirrors that stare

& make you aware of whose bellies
leave the half-trees torn & twisted
I do not think things through
when I take to the river

ours is the wedding-garment
ours the shroud
ours the movie of a shadow play
as quick as if the vision touched you

kinder

kite & wilderness what
joy to measure
in a cave
her silken flanks w/
garlands drest then
bang & we emerge
with barfly remorse

a whisper dies
the meaning of her black eyes
the richness of her manner
the slightly dishonorable past

in the day she feeds birds
but hasn't got
the holes half full
what difference does it make
if her firmament spills into the room

on the french coast
I will stand a long time
recovering pleasure
the heavy surface
of what was said
by the oral to
the written
indecipherable cause
neither arnold's intersection
nor whitman's simple folk

we'll walk through the valley
through the herbs & sweet-cress
though I will feel lost
waters from mountain springs
trail between love & state
a confirming skin
a temple to colonize

my probe into your anus
ovalness where my love
is the age-old rock star
becomes an autobiography

a male is not less nor more
a flow of clear liquid
official greeter
a loss that will not seem so

dancing on your breast amorous & slippery
I was ten when you buried me
& the gates of the body
with two cracked handles

secret writing
trails from the heaven you create

soul

so shall
my mistress sun
herself
give space to voices
when love swears she's made of truth

lemons feed themselves
her joy to be alive

power can abolish
these little things
& in any case govern
shade & gentle breezes
the grass on which we sit or lie
like some sort of altar
slick with lemon

I never talked to you
in the dales of arcady
so take what
wouldn't stay green there
the poor lemon

frame

children naked as
the old woman mountain
hang strips of back meat
& sip elemental tea
as if they could
pull dying into a dance

& having assumed the
thick skin of this town
the salt rock's face to seaward
singing river & wood
rivermouth vocable blood beat
etymology of a kiss

I will keep you company
& penetrate the pavilions
even if finally all is done
upon the tomb & we are here
as on a plane
to laugh at the miracle

like a ladder
where tramps are kings
ruby throat of this republic
unwinds its winding path
come take my hand & see
if lilies can be lily white

when the proud son returns to earth
wanting to know
child of its flesh
happy genius of the household
his book being gift of
all this together
supposing it was actual
like pomegranates splitting
on the banks of a stream
where mermaids sing
with yellow drawn shades
or moon's sickle
this earthly hell makes
all feel better
burning & gunning in america
& dusk a gash of neon
a flowery tale of something
upright & earnest
like the folds of a bright girdle
astride the dreary intercourse
of daily life
spring like a perhaps
wheelbarrows similarly plastered
a valorous legend
for the church of hygiene
the blank bulk of us
& a language to dream in

snake with no hiss
no olives no fasting
day after day
the bone china of

man's calamity
yet I wouldn't
doubt that under its wrist is still
a pulse stabbed & shot
untapped & untappable
where the families all disperse
to their kitchen wars
& the leaves bid spring adieu
& the studio guests
play their clapboard hopscotch
with a brass coin
& a burlap veil
dying before we had time even
to be stripped of foliage

small iridescent flies
furies of complicated
precession
gutter glare
earth in adolescence
trying to rebuild
my exhortations
embers need poking
heart & head unheard
& grey as
a magic button
in the bronx
where one all-loving
motion flares
at the center
of a great yellow flower

pastoral

now I hand
what tears I have
to you for language which
on this scene impress
a blue solitude
of stars

the real world
or what the public understands
arranged by men with
pears and crosses
can't forget the cool evening
air kisses rush of blood

& you who
have killed to own your
joy what pleases you more
than your back against the
jungle where nothing grows
& nothing keeps

ah let us be true
to an orange frontier
beyond the frieze
on my knees with both feet
you'll find you've come
to yourself through centuries

arraignment of the lover
of meadows & woods
on this exact spot
where the little stream

flows with bodies of
horses & men

war and then war
voice of
its own birth
this river
this concrete river
I am beast of beasts

as a blue vase
sheds rainbows on grass
the shafts of yesterday's pain
that human vices wake in us
delicate & strangely proud
a motion & a spirit that impels

we are making a future today
with rapid unanimous hands
echo of steel sounds grating sky
the eyes of my bones
sing to the hand the mantra
through a mist of completeness

in autumn we bought
for the natives peace
in a beggar's half-etched squat
happiness on a wave
coffee black coffee
since I left you

fair play

if in your eye your smile
or your feet open doors
& blue sky
in mind of man
then the wall
with its dizzy raptures
fierce as a dog
lapping for action
leaves me to
feast on myrtles &
noise of my own voice
my own
publishing stream
seems a snapshot
of torment
of fire & weight
affording nothing
somber pleasure
asleep or it malingers
to taste the slabs
of salt the ingots
of copper intimacy

tell me you are me
& I believe you
veteran of
wine cracking the dirt
tried & true trite twisting of
raw silk into the revenant
lift her spirit
attune her voice
show no mistake in reasoning

leveller of periplum
the hermit sits alone
saying tombstones & music

I believe you have found
a spell to draw me out
I thought every secret was
you when you don't exist
how do you speak how know
the image of what
I'd wanted
steeped brewed & spent like a
dry leaf trembling on a wall

participants came in a
cluster of dialects
high tones low & mid
whose prospects & pride
woods & copses get lost in
layers of murmur &
slashed worlds
certain half-deserted streets
to the planet floor
the tiny fuselage of a vine

at twenty I tried
but over me a face
I'm surprised to find
soft sentiment & salutes
purge the shame of being born
more love from him at
19 than ever from

the unseen wing
impossibly intricate
the magnetic curses
why not
persona al mundo
rig a little hammock
then retrace your steps

st patrick st mark
furnished with
a stained mattress
even the bawds of euphony
burp the millennial sorrows
into a mantle of summer
no sound like the dolphin-torn
grief &
faith knowing
something gone
through the open gate
streets full of people
& she sat
muttering holy whys

I used to go & visit him
his lone darkness opposing
& corrupting
like a proper gypsy
like a master craftsman
& there were gates
to see us through
to sleep buddhalike
in his hallway

the subterranean path
the ants & pebbles
the vein of will

what guards what
purity of melting
my mouth sewn shut
with an alphabet of tokens
unoriginal angels
vs. the sole known
photograph of him up the hill
very full very successful
& under his ribs
the heart of his people
surrounded by beautiful curious
breathing laughing flesh

no addled keeper of yesterday's
magic can startle this pain
& make it move & live

your impudence protects you from
an empty heart
shadow of a blackbird
every time I'd turn my head

filled with literary
peers & dukes &
all the sweeping train
rung after rung
amid the mirrored shapes
of country people

lights never go out
the woods on our side
eyes that I love
night resonance recedes
night walker's song
half full of cold
every day it dies

affective expression

those who know nothing but
ways to develop
effective outlets sing these

hopeless days
overspread with phantom light

still afraid of
yesterday's garbage
you do not answer

o pious one
standing on the marble steps
your wild passions breathing
utmost sorrow into still becoming

you are no help
in this landscape
surrounded by your books
beneath a bright alcove
which smells of rose & honey &
unassailable custom

& would it have been worth while
if however inspired & properly
approved my lays
were consumed of
mouths & tongues only

to die in the gutter
in full regalia
like a lazarus of the street
beautiful
as an alcohol lamp
shed from the bosom of

the crescent moon
watch it grow
into a thieves' market

I have a notion of
the drowned face
always staring
a woman in housedress & slippers
window with the light
idleness brings

gay fancy cheerful eyes
pitchers of honey
shiploads of spice
& the sun a flame-white disc
my way of entrapping myself
when blackbirds fly out
as if their souls converged to
test their worth

I collect dying men
the french horn silhouette
souls in motion
your me was all in all
I cannot paint it

or make this fortress assume
your landscape with quiet sky

box of stone
statues on her head
not as a humble citizen speck
but in natural perfect attitude
bent arm curved neck

may it stun sybil into prophecy
like a tree saying this is memory
this is sensation
happening elsewhere
in order to reach you

let's begin at the beginning
diaper pins in my fist
where else do we do
soundings but here

lily song
willing & yielding
quivering when it comes time for you to
lower your eyes

I had to kill you
in that rhythm
& now sex is what
does it for me
& for you
suspended in sleep
skin so fine
or finally dreamed

the train clicked & sighed

I want to be buried in it
like the severed head
of an outlaw
like the doctor
of past existence
sculptor of private needs
fact paralyzed by fact

from self-awareness
embedded in situ
to end up dreams touching
where we lie sleeping
under a bridge

there were so many birds
the bushbank
grew still as we urged
our paper-weight hearts
our cheek maps of outworn days
through shining trees
mistaking cultural history for a
sensual tale our
bloodshot drunkard's eye
seemed to give
a summary to the plants

dailies on the corner
on every side of
the making of heroes
manchildness &
tricycle treads scribble
the nuclear son
born of woman
man born of woman

before I begin again
put me where
I can't hear the plans
like sparrows in a cloudless
starless lake of blue

kernel

not god but a swastika
like a veil over the
author's headstone
a tale less deep & loud
than signs & fists
always empty like this

drink up your lovecries &
memorized chaucer
songs hoarded in exile
naked omphalos pierced
lily of lacquer

if you should dip your hand
suffuse yourself in
untrammeled pastures
in confusion I return home
to the current that makes
the machinery crackle

the grass sleeps by the river
like a young journalist
things looming oddly in him
populist states & rich republics

& when lightnings flash
& rocks cry out to us
over a brown plain
like a great spider's back
in tanto potuit populo esse
even myrtle leaves curl & shrink

attic shape but
wary attitude
freed from brassiere
tempered with delight
ghosts are walking
body at auction
the taste made deities
hiss & snort

ceremonial certainty

sharp swish of a branch
& a hospital of
grammar supplies
we receive but what we give

bury an urn with
not even a card
or chance to decline
a notion of sin now vanished

copulating beneath a full moon
those blessed structures
plot & rhyme
plant themselves with me here

glorious green
tamborine harmonica mandolin
spray-painted outpourings
the ground dry as wood

& even if it could be a harbor
let your tongue savor
the wind melting
light from an olive oil lamp

this is how it came about
preferring any future
love to this present
I could hardly speak

of day breaking for you
the eddies & curlicues
the mule-tongued flowers
the pear's red flesh

what chanted in darkness &
throat-bracketed light
nightmare of the I
lying alone

what stranger
scaled the wall
as we passed in the street
light of a prison lamp

that bedeviled memory
at home in unhappiness
with the air of one dying
birds quietly singing

engraved figure guarding
the intaglio self
how sovereign was my touch
I wore your love & pity

nothing

you are the presence of
what were suburbs in 1955
white nymph anterior attention
no words in you but
lying in-state
like a flower
like a golden sleeve

god's assistance
the imminent sting
it was a book
thousands of readers
changed in the continuation

the world is round but
what will be brought to us
can't be remembered
an unknown source
winced when you said it

panting & kissing
to coax into light
that certain
desperate branding
iron hot noon
singular like your
heart with rejoicing

a child sleeps
in a pile of doeskin
snowman rooted
yearning to respond

you touched her sleeping breasts
forgot where you were
freed from beat & measure

but wilting
could a dream send up
that refreshing breeze
that turns out to sea
& eventually sleeps

blind

dressed in your new blue suit
each rock a word
razored for a fight
over cities
beneath a moon
above the sports-caster's booth

technology & future directions
hawked on the street
knowledge becomes him
he likes it that way
brings everything to his
self that lay

where crowded skyscrapers could
use the vacant brain
death comforts &
croons & shuffles &
seeing it pass
conveys as much as a poem

he swears she's made of truth
says how full of light we are
while sleeping
a pollen-tinted crack
when all one has is darkness
haven in a heavenless stare

scent of resin in these
pebbles last night's
rain uncovered

she has fitted up her hair
under a hand-me-down
with bows in every color
bodies beneath frail cover
silent as sleeping earth
a sigh & a little groan that
linger in the thigh

stamp

we stood together & together
longed for a native language
a legacy of oppression
a grass plot where
marble men reach the trees

the canopy
the furniture of home
of a country
connected by
possessing & receiving

rain water
slips over
spear-tipped walls
take my love with its
chorus of exclusions

one of many
glimmering out in the bay
could I hear their anguish
in this broken book
this single step

even if not everyone
has the cheerful faith
I had when I was young
sometimes the past sees
you etched in light

an impedance a dance
a hand you reel out of sight
out of the book
& old grudges
time has ticked advice around

use your science well
& you'll walk through shadows
unafraid of dying
tongue refined from oil & stone
become a living soul

a wall of power
transforms despair
to cocaine heaven
as the century crosses its
blackstockinged legs

caught up and estranged
I share your strength &
cease to be me
merely a grammar
sitting next to you in bed

words chosen randomly
have a right to clear sight too
turning judgments to sneers
all vanities at once
congealed on earth

the stars are not
philosophers
to avenge this poverty
or the bird of eros
you dropped from

alleys of imagination
like a silver weed
giving birth again
meeting back where we started
in the torture room

speech

I understand
from under the ocean
I understand
he laughs
marked
looking on
muttering gods
& love (they pretend)
& rainbow
saying I do I do
not here in the
concrete of course
but in a book
a talismanic strum
your beggar's finger
a coming to sacrifice

I have wished myself
something different
but you you're the dirt
under the royal nails
you'll be back for more
elevated thoughts
& sense sublime all
these expressions of
the well-made man

stop

fast music
sweet token
of untainted
interpretation
righteous & wise
a mansion of forms
inflamed
a new thing that thinks
two by two
sound of a planet
in communication
the walk & the waltz
expected or
feared now
consumed
as melts the
sugar in the tea

spangles two hundred sixty years old
yours for the taking
bring your self home to your
self enter the garden

as if it were all
mine shall we sail
round & round
shoulders & beard scapula &

engine an engine
with thin fingers
fit instrument
for a world reclaimed from beasts

& the fiction of
a voice beyond boundaries

days feel like marches
form after formless form
back & forth
so various so beautiful so new

setting down these lines
to punish you

pomp
all that man is
a breath a chance at
ripples calling
on a vacant lot at sundown after work

please

come up
draw us under
with reactions like
kindness & love
devotion & pause

once its name was
on walls
on a chaos
of walls

take a
salamander's mien
madman &
woman &
blackbird

faint echo of the
puppet
in your hand

to undo the
folded lie of
where we have been
together
taxi cabs at night
I want to be
a sacrament
set forth
this evening
our birds
green again

but I see
we are at war
& the jabberwock's
eyes light
the fields of oil

our globe lay
billions of years
without plant animal or angel
but now what pipes
& timbrels

busy sylphs
around their darling
submarine
what didn't they do
to entertain you

dare

all my days of
happiness & wonder
serenity pickled
in a jar of self

books religion time visible as
solid atmosphere
earth spirit after spirit
wine of sloth

between arpeggio & arbor
some dread event impends
tiny hand flexing a wing
its head pale yellow

this glob is the globe
young fellow hoeing corn
sleigh-driver guiding horses
free of moral law

priests mean to stomp
with cold hard mouth
the houses we once occupied
that faded into evening

a path straight out
of the rock-side
moving with perfect balance
& from under a rock her

sister laughing
I could see
her sharp shoulder bones then
years went by with an iron clank

the auctioneer doesn't
really know his business
rubbing memory's structure
that no rampart excludes

aboard a sun-flooded schooner
she'll turn up in spires
& keep the mailman busy
though we won't be living

mayflies

so june can hold
the codicil-ready cables
& brilliant cliffs of england
we'll pick a sea-fruit
with no leaves
& trot off to the darkest part
of the woods

wake up & come out now
in an allegory
in both positive & negative repose
dark deep & absolutely clear
any posture you can read in
your countless lives with
countless embodiments

I'm a stolen car
I know this now
lurid & more melodious than
surf among rocks
a circular corpse
I'll make you aware of
summer & winter

the greatest charm of
grass is this gently sloping head
like you threw off rooftops
white & violet flight with
a glass slipper & a helpless blue rose
but you must first of all show
what you have under your coat

perhaps that I was questioned
between words made a torquing
& they hide their faces
behind houses
behind masters from america
I turn to listen from
birch & ash

leaf-fringe about our shape
you make an account for
the soft-palmed land owners
yesterday's yawning cure
place without a
pang void

nothing to say or
play in this presence
& by so doing
you have imagined it
melodies echo that voice
& nudge my tongue awake

fan

across a desert of stars to drink the world
wishing the same splendor the same
road ahead the same
light of a naphtha lamp
we kiss belly to belly
in a phantom colony

this plastic death in a can
is no more certain than
no more elevating than
rosewood

all I have are
vague embankments
fleece drums & public flutes
no transportation
no rice-filled buddha frown

head & arms folded
over our wonder & turning
toward a window that should speak
frail as a bosom
unwrinkling from cocoon for flight
perpetual dreaming
circulating through
police & prison & tranquilizers
what a terrible waste of
sweat & pursed-lip imaginative
literary political thinking

words have been written
out of love's best habit
advancing through
exile & activism
then the wind blows
breathing in & out

when i walk there
walks beside me
a reptile as
reticent as
I am vocal
as silent as
I am awake
when I protest
my innocence my
reputation it
laps up some
shit & when I'm
scared to death
it scoots into the
maw just to feel
its final shudder
heels like the faithful
turning as I
turn seeing
what I see
when we two walk
there in the
breach

coin

icicles fill the window
where pulpy red
men meet gravely
sweet soft pipes playing
my designs concentrating

the child feels
the hypocrisy of
these words deceit
as when winds of winter tear
an oak naked

I am no longer sure
I am the two eyes
screwed to my
head black & glossy as a
spider's web

I have unfinished encounters
& hope to wait & see
what triumph is
untwisted from the last
strands of man

I lived in hopes
the judgement was
a forgotten sensation
but how many choirs sang
that weary song

purchase

years of
life passing
green as grass

the old love or
pleasure of a new
heartless mood

round the sad church
& youth that
grows old in it

they will say
this love is greater
than the fashionable pretense

like shoots of red bamboo
blood showed
a cymbal on their necks

spirit mountain
boulevards & mazes
& something is lost

but death is
full of moon & blessing
voices with thumbs

nothing matters but
surprise I thought
& the dangers that attend

translators
they that the tribes call
among porcelain among

the stream that flows
round me like a vine
surface without grace

muttering at dawn
delineated politically
conservative soul an actor

forgetfulness is
such sweet singing
& tonight a clown

sneaks out of a painted mouth
into the armed struggle for
your attention span

escape

I love the breath
within you or within me
bone & marrow
a good human
soil on the skin
always in the same spot

when I see standards
gold or purple opposing
aficionados critics cultured laborers
man's body at auction
once forgotten you're a
world aflame

the exact expression I cannot recollect
in a glass coach
woods tall as waves
dark salt clear moving utterly free
flowing one after another
they hear they all hear

against the health of mankind
on skulls & bones of his people
& what shows as a branch
as winter has my absence
a spectacle & nothing strange
& the murder left undone

when a child's forehead full of red torments
resists in a way outside its own interest
music will play on a cold summer night
& what we imagine knowledge to be—
boys rehearsing their parts—
becomes these faces along a bar

I's I've known already
a simple economy denoting rimbaud
what made him think
there was only one nothing
he loved me I see now
without revelation

gourds arranged in a circle
like a cause
a cause loud enough to say
god forbid you make me your slave
your chest will ache immediately
somewhere else til you come know it

lift & drop

you will be more likely to find
my thoughts food for life
when these wild bourgeois ecstasies mature
& no one inhabits your world

I welcome the shroud
made of sticks mop for a wig
never having courted
staying out of danger

I will be true to
the advisability of this house
the settling of station
pears wadded in cloth

thinking she thinks me young
with death on our panel
horns & humps
all spit & electrified hum

when our elbows & swords
walk away a step or two
neglecting their own concerns
to render service to others

a sensual ear from somewhere else
impromptu warrior billyclub
complexities of mire & blood
begin to shrug off resemblances

a diagonal slant to the rosebushes
a rock a river a tree
not too many things like
sapphire light

shall prevail
or even disturb
while rocking on a deck
how we come to understand things

cupid

I have seen your painted
autumn reckless & resolved
yet perpetually under siege

the windows of the town
are hornets' nests
afraid of being stung

what an aranda uses words for
hoarse flute floating
over a well meaning body

to be great
what would greatness be
a blackbird flying

a passage from proverbs he chose
marked like a quail's crown

no one exists alone but the
attorney churning misery

chains of the bondsmen dragging
as the curiously-glowing guard dogs bark

our would-be cities fall
& then things bloom

ever more hurt than substance will
accrue to you I say thru locks of curled wire

then feel the heart within me fall & flutter
the voice an artificial hermetic closet

a resting-place full of summer
sounds & scents

fear sticking up its head
& ticking as if earth were finally ready

dream thing

I behaved like what I am
a magic lantern of rack & screw
weaving passion for new beginnings
come to after a while on the ground

something surging & dying continuously
a desire to wring light from clouds
for today who can afford to drink calmly
& verbalize self back into place

your pure circling thoughts express
space & time accurately while
universities swallow themselves &
imagine the killing over again

see this simple urn
no storm disturbs its flame
dance steps flooding streets
& the gust that carried you over the rocks

there are caves or caverns of some kind up ahead
one for each of my companions
we'll find out if any paradise was
selected from our list and get
the photos coming except
in a rage to leap and lash out
with double no treble high-octane
whisky all nodded agreement &
touched the bandage noting how
it might be to rule by music
let's play he barked
& sat back redundantly to enjoy
a new computer program for every body sent

suppose the rest of the message
mixed with a long slender needle
& an elective silence when your seed
breathless mouths may summon
brush of prickly leaves & taste of coarse weeds
a rasping thomas jefferson still lives
invokes a muse of satire like
fools resisting arrest petty griefs have their
quantities & tempers & mexico bares
its teeth in retrospect a thing
of higher import I say in words
of pindar than any business come alive
coarse & strong cunning as love with
fruits & sweets & its armor of black rubber
it is an awful pipe for no-tone ditties
ditties for titties & lots of golden honey
all daisy rings & lingering on a purposed undertow
talking & reading & chanting & dubbing & turning
& hovering over your name on a flyleaf look
lost ponies with something like
men & women coming on
can it be crushed into extracts which mystic
indians faun & spend good money for
tortoise here & elephant unite & swing
from the clapper or cool spring
in the desert where housekeepers
perform upon a lonesome wild
you'll drink her milk &
have no word for the pleasure

today I'll bring you to my riverside
& we'll sit down at some quiet spot
& add names to the list
those who could cloud in lazy strokes
the red marble of a slight night shower
questions of your presence on earth
of dramatic collaborations & naked acts
illusions eyes that will never close
you think you ought to be going on dead
this mocking beauty portends
tamquam commictae spurca saliua lupae
what woman god hero what virgin man's
delicate bibliophile sex lives in this dump
with head uncovered & cosmetic powers
& spider lilies in the shadow
the sea of faith from where we sit
a glass eye for the tongue there are
no words for the endearments I dream they
carry us under the waters of the world
I have to go back you understand
back to inhale her milky aroma
in solitude in fear in pain or grief
rotating under stars & moon & sun
when my life is sleeping
& breath & breath
fold into one another

matheme

equations encircling
clio who is
clinging to the path
amphoral mound kiss
potion whiffling
through cork-wood
my joy is the same as
an aromatic astringent
at midnight on an emperor's
pavement flitting
to exhale & back again

towers stand &
various rings appear
tangent to the brook
tan feet then goat feet
older in myth
& unwearied by service
friends places reflections
recollections of dancing
give them back
to the sullen
night air

libation of benzene
set in the sprinkle
dress designs
pride of man
calming & excellent
for the soul
fuzzy from medication

fingers along my waist
in self intoxication
suffixum in summa
me memini esse cruce
cellular flesh of the
stone bridegroom
night of love
prostrate dawn
that time has past
waiting for a
boat to come

difference

the time we passed
with your uncle
on the mantle
wild fruit trees bent
with confused alarms
doubts lingering like
old men bald & rich
preparing faces to meet
the face of lasting summer

paradise sparks brighter
combing the white hair
of these dishonest decades
with an evening light
a grave & awkward mask
being the manner of death
as is the landscape
to a blind man's eye
knowing their tongue
leaves will fall &
it is going to snow

obsessing on our private lives
your eyes upon
colour upon
suffusion of light
rafters listen
to the singing
to the apprehensive breath
a fraction of a flower

the old romantic lie
here to break
new ground
good-natured
native-born

all in one
flesh a revolutionary
force that
can avail
from guzzling blood
jeans & an old t-shirt
all the aching joys

even your voice was
supposed to be here
but not invited
consumed like a
readymade soft
yielding minds
moving through the
absence of deep woods
& lofty cliffs
as once I returned
in late summer
with my love

in the clear fountain of eternal day
on that green light that lingers in the west
when our bodies have become terrain
for resolving birdsongs & crickets
a raven with dark falling wing stripped bare
sent my soul abroad in the eye of a blackbird

maybe the choir sings tunes without words
& willow mirrors fleck the deep song sound
a dwelling-place for the dreamer's naivete
make your living with flesh & you'll be
shredding grass until the whimpering flowers
sail through all the parts together

a lamp is only a sign of glass all thinking
things all objects of thought why don't you come
today a hand is on the gate today when I gain
creative change in a future alive & bent to a helix
peace past walking is like love & the rock that
made me weep for myself

the people gathered round the royal carrion
agitated even worn away at any rate truant
tokens but no organs & conflicts all over the globe
unrolling endlessly more & more scroll
that serene & blessed mood
as it were earth's breast milk

I'd been sitting all morning in a poem & I petted it
& put it under the house to make it more lonely
contentment sprinkled over a veiled rider
who claims himself the exclusive heaven
of a book thought wicked spanning forty winters
besieged an appendage of work stemming from

vocabularies that might express what you & I
battled within sight of reason the same slight slight
the same simple negative that gave
us india dying under its ancient truck
seeking ways out of french poetic enlightenment
and the cantors singing in the half-light

me

come taste this
fruit little gunner
he said
sailing like
a blind fool
his fake neutral air
drowned in a book
a crook in town
to repent but
it was too late
in the cold living room
to take off
his tie
to touch
the strange lumps
beneath the pine

blackbirds boozy
the emperor's drunken
soldiery abed
seen over &
over same old
sea same old
sound
shrill & summery
that even in
slumber caused
his cheek to
glow every man every

woman carries
this filament
life predestined
surly & interested like
the coming-on of rain

I infect with
meaning something exact
as reality's dark
dream when the
lanterns go out
the matching skullcap
& map of brain
his peat-brown head

music from a far off room
like these
mountains this
infinite movement
mingling with all
sound all
thought the dull
sobbing draft
that moans the
image of your
public self

hoarse from
days drinking
anticipating a message
to the armies of
those engulfed
in black water

why does his mind
envy reed & hawthorne
is it to have
a point again
arranging & changing
& placing the eye
again dehumanized

he has a dozen hands
& pollackesque friends
to make germinate
language as
a choir of worms
saying names
like money spent
on misconceptions
whose silver cargo
vision banished

when they pulled
me from the sack
I reeked of you
I defiled you
the ways you live
your secrets of life
joined in spite
in the attics of
old houses
proud full of verse
what little town
by river or sea
gates the flaming
word that is yourself

what pursuit what
struggle to escape
cuffed & clawed
but not crying
what wilderness future
light of our knowledge
yields this penelope
who would reduce
our banter to
rules of probability

planted on a star-lit
golden bough
the necessary
the tap
the tap that
nothing satisfies
but self remembering
self its former height
its discordant strains
its brain that ink
may mark with vine-boughs

he lay
back eyes closed
the eyes of
youth to roll
it is a journey he said
of the curious
not to be wed forever
but like one who watches
down the row of
statues to see
the divine nimbus
a music
a rose colored
dress

we took our seats
& ghosts & armies
came down

green butterflies
from the age of love

shadows of
earthly vehicles

the sea of air
the perfumed
agony of a trance

you who gave me
my first you

you where I
is a roomful of clothes

flame that no
fuel feeds nor
steel has lit

flame from
before the surprise
before affection &
shame

your body

your loves

your farewell

agon

collective agency even at home
for elegy elephants
riding seaward
bobbin bound in mummy-cloth

slight is subject slight is praise
a fatted wanderer through wood
a broken manifold
a certain time selected & assured

I loosen myself pass freely
as a little child
while about the shore
those that cling ripen

suauiolum dulci dulcius ambrosia
cut to the knot-core of his heart

commander

sir or madam president
vice-president & treasurer
horror is but one of your
charming fripperies

hand-picked from a red matte
this house of the great witch
this moment of life & flood
& flattery out of the bathroom now

I'm dressed as a rose
to entice & burn
to disturb your universe
as trumpets join chorus

no matter who it is
in ocean light or dark
that old age wastes
sitting in the sun alone

where you cross
to the temple of artemis
a creek-washed stone
coalesces with history

death to be sure but somehow
like redbirds
miracle bird or golden hawk
teeming river & tree

elegy

revisited soul
refusing to believe
a former self's
airport rituals
a purple ribbon
on the bed
till we are
all recolonized
it is a war
for this world

to keep it
to keep
the it
not to think
not to remember
not to discover
the opal light
along the bank

plots of cottage-ground
orchard-tuft
eye-fringe
iris of
guardian of
my small silences

true brain in its folds
inside the skull-frame
lorry of passion
& lapsed intention

who's imagined
seeing
& seeing
behind
gossip from the ghost

solidity of bark
leaf or wall
made me
dream of happiness
cradled in these
arms & eyes

& the temple
in the mountain
smoke-filled
wants accuracy
wrong in the mind
& in the bowels
the groans
of trampled men
dumb in the
bright morning

eagle shadow
blackbird whistle
center that causes action
cobbled out of a
milky way

lover of my
youth & age
arrives
working odd jobs
a figure
in a photograph

I hear the pulse
somewhere
of my elocutionary
mass my
animated dust
a little drunk
on shadow wine
shrivelled by frost
having lain too long
in this language

we talk of decline
with some urgency
but a passing police
car pulls the
picture I have of you

the gulf
between planets
where you
had to pass
or touch or
rest on my arm
ever so lightly a
camera

bread

I have known
the breath you store
behooved fiduciarily to
have nothing to say

in a little room without
discourse without
even language
but a pistol shape

your head no sooner
from the natives turns
than fictional bones
begin to ache

ashes on your head
violet indestructible tree
your thick branches
burn with misery

element

then soul
come back to
rails we rode
when language
whispered aloud
it's hard to quarrel
sinking into dust
soft cities we
made in three days

glad

history is the dream of what
we were too ill to teach

affections gently lead us on
but sometimes everything I say
wants to hunt the dead leaves

what is wind what is it
pieces of a past rising out of
the master's name
dead-beaten in effort on effort

the dire one desired
sign of something more
cracking a heart into features
collective experience come
to a stop in company with evening

I sit in some dive in total immersion
tape recorder of imprecise gestures
but outside the red gates none
respond to this framework of frailty

locusts chant out of dunghills
for future years & so I dare to hope
for a pitchy darkness with gods

beneath ghastly statues
all I desire ends every road

crab

---

the ones who kill
kill & go freely
same in all nations
point after point

each of us descendant of
some past rage reviving
the great assembly line
with its din of exquisite screams

it is as if the dull substance of
flesh were thought & portentous
natures spoke beside the river before
being buried in their chains

& the god
rode dumbly over connecticut
a young kid full of nothing

the language of your former heart
has descended to your legs

I promised to follow
these obscure birds
or any image of
error bred in the bone

mass produced intellectuals link struggles
in mercy & medicine to rock piles of despair
while hope & self-esteem cull & quaintly toil
with geographic robots constellated around a son

my hand or rather my heart lapped
strength from wheelbarrows & pushed
new vocabularies on laureled wisdom
capitulating to the intruder just to observe

the onrushing host loops thought as a green sprig
hatband concentrate perfect in tragic sounds
like a songless beaten-down man with sores
on his insides an endlessly dirty old thing

no citizen or police would bleed to death
if you could think in your own language
& no past is deeper than the dark-brown gardens
of peeping flowers like bogart as he winces

gown me in a robe so light & long I disappear
I'll know but one & here he lies unveiled
light of a lamp & dark rosemary
original members of this empty fold

snatch chatter

I have & still will
dance naked in
word or sigh

let those scorn who never
let the joy within
dally with death

do not desert us
come & tend
this last unnumbered mile

our life alone will make two or three
more rushed resilient word-sounds
before running home to mother

could one imagine
that these desires
were a kind in glass & a cousin

charming genius with modest manners
the air smelled so strong of codfish the house
had undue influence on one of us

knowing words are all we dream

token

it is in your walk & carriage
neck turn flex of the waist
wherever nature lead
so balmy & serene
foot after foot like a
gypsy ancestor
riffling through the
river I
an old man
calling to quail &
pheasant but
pockets full of
you in mind's eye

ivy strangling trees
a light a glory
a luminous cloud
what dictators do
after removal from earth

in atom-bomb light

velvet cords
of the museum

motion

quickly move quickly
that the chaff might fly &
grain lie sheer

strained scales
of a useless beauty
I used to call your black telephone

I as though tipping a pitcher of milk
my song that no tree can hear
no butterfly no ant can bridge

winged to be winged by thought
who's ever left naked
with elevations to be celebrated

don't hide your face
sit down with me
in this blue light

green growth

an old man sits knitting
curses & thoughts
listening on alert for
my farther my more than myself

I'm going to let another
sing for me now
heads together eye to eye
fossilled in our separate stone

may this storm be a mountain-birth
lobster pots & masts scattered
host to species long departed

not mine not ours
but like a walk in the garden
when nothing else will do

—New Orleans, September 2006 - April 2007

Coda for Federico García Lorca

for Peter Gizzi

From the Manzanares east to Retiro
men chant inside suits, sensing
the rush, acid curves and martinis.
November milk scours the plateau from rocks,
and kids debunk escalators & perspectives.

People: no one is dedicated,
no one carries the river,
no one ambles lost over granaries,
no one assembles the legends for the play.

From the Manzanares east to Ventas
men lunch on industry
see judges bring the faun, wringing
proposals of circumnavigation
as cellos disembark to points east of Texas,
places of business, emptied of elevation.

People: no one is detained,
no one inquires or nudges,
no one rumbles or reflects
that the crude armadillo still trembles.

Winds of lunatic salvation
rotate over tundra and silence
as death adjudicates memory
east of attitudes so level they're unafraid.

Madrid descends,

Madrid deactivates east of mirth.

As angels levitate, occult and labial,

as vision predicts neither dirt nor virtue,

as the suave terror of anemones mandates,

the knee of our soul moans. Feed her slowly, Federico
       García Lorca.

These decades of fear your borrowed lines dematerialize:

& we kneel to the humble and pained gestures of loons,

& we kneel to the muscles of a polio victim,

& we kneel to voices under columns of censors.

Ancient hermetic code of need,

key and jewel of the effort to feel,

coin of sex altered for a grudge,

enemy of satire,

enemy of vitality,

a man with long curls drops his burden of light.

& the knee of our soul moans, her vital measure

that in mountains of carbon announced the ferocious

son, a bastard but royal in demeanor, coming up the river

with aging comrades to ponder and to pick up

the political colors of an ignorant leopard.

& the knee of our soul moans, adept at salvage,
       mechanized,

its humor sold in markets. Feed her slowly, Federico
       García Lorca.

Story for the aztecs,

anxious hope laid bare,

silent and rational as elemental force,

temperate in those places of lost chauffeurs,

Garibaldi on the platforms of the ocean,

those miracles, Federico García Lorca, you personify.

Tambourine so easy! Tambourine! He's despondent,
toothed & bearded & luminous– he casts
rubies north into the arena,
without ado or grief he's adamant,
combing gates & combing serpents–
those miracles, Federico García Lorca, those miracles–
turbines and liquid, carnal parts fusing
into the boat of mortal delight doñas adore.

Tambourine so easy! Tambourine! Did we tender
a punctual and soothing delusion,
a qualified mirror come to maintain
union labor? We savor our gasoline
as the soul pants for obligation,
and those aching for judgment are judged by fools.

Kneel to buses & cars, those obvious arrangements,
neither planned nor obscure, but submerged in old lies,
neither body nor head,
neither curved as a comma nor like ants in soap,
the leaden old mariners approach & trample
meaning as lost inertia or the equine bells of terror.

You brought the denuded queen's fire, came into
this town and swept away the red stains of algae,
pardoned age with the camellia of your myth,
& gave a last look to an equator now occluded.

Now we adjust to humble endings, suits of lights
salvaged from the sand of that maniacal war that killed
            you.
Hell sent tender prayers down into the aether,
and the queen of debits repented in your aura.

Agony, agony, self fermented in self.
This is the mountain and the meaning, agony, agony:
those mulattoes seen disembarking to relocate in capitals,
the guerilla passing around a million rated germs,
the rich men donning their theory
passing moribund & infected,
neither vital nor noble, neither lurid nor sacred.

Padding down the sick century, your descent
is slower than coral or celestial nudes,
your amorous seraphim rock the tempo
like brides aquiver among lost rams.

For Exxon we level the voice, young Federico García
        Lorca,
contrary to the events we describe
but numb to their implication,
not contrary to the much lauded vistas of the novel
or the obscurity of romance,
not contrary to solitary locations or locutions
that can bribe a scholar or a prostitute,
not contrary to hunger in the mirrored village,
can a man with hunger quote labels and silence?
Pain is contrary to us, marimbas of the suicides,
incarnate tutelage and pensive immunity—
manufactured for airplanes, we sing
an amorous repartee crowned with algebra.

Contrary to the simple, to the days of lost mysticism,
goats sucking myrtle in a margin or a vein.
Contrary to the simple,
take the ferry to the North Sea,
or fly into Havana,
there's a shuttle to Mexico,
a fast train to Cádiz,
a flight to Sevilla,

cancer of New York,
flowers in Alicante,
over-development in Portugal.

Miracles of the mountain, assassins of the moment,
enclaves of the movement forced to drink coca-cola,
abandon the plazas with fever and abandon
or embrace the yokes beyond their circuits.

No hero's welcome– the myth
man deserved is over,
and groups of flowers rise in a barely felt circle.
No halting question– alert
to those confounded, those burros,
those classic cars, those senior ladies, those supplicants
of the subtle ports of the bacchanal,

& you, Federico García Lorca, did your friends in Granada
convert your barbed glance into the last alien birds?
Have the necessary options you laid out
been cancelled like valor & grace in conception?
Or do they lie dormant, like lost senses,
as the dance of mirrors agitates a private and privatized
America? She arranged her mechanical lament
merely to clear the air for a future
of quiet flowers, as letters told actors about death,
& a kneeling negrito announced a lost band of gold,
love yielding the reins to data and spirit.

–Madrid, 20-27 July, 2004

Notes

transfixion is the culmination of a procedural project that began with *look the universe is dreaming* in 2002, the primary difference between the two being that the sorting of the literary quotations is much less random– i.e. involves more subjective agency– in this newer work.

Every word or phrase in the book ought perhaps to be in quotation marks, rather like Alice Notley's *The Descent of Alette.* I leave it, however, to the reader to sort out the densities of "reference" and whether, in each instance, what is occurring is quotation, allusion, homage, parody, echolalia, unconscious mirroring, plagiarism or, indeed, normal speech.

Translations of lines from Catullus:

non cessasti omnique excruciare modo– (12)
and to torture him in every manner

non si densior aridis aristis
sit nostrae seges osculationis– (23)
not if the harvest of our kissing
were thicker than the ripe ears of corn

in tanto potuit populo esse– (48)
could there not be found in all these people

tamquam commictae spurca saliua lupae– (83)
as if my spit were as filthy as a she-wolf's urine

suffixum in summa me memini esse cruce– (85)
I hung impaled on the top of the cross

suauiolum dulci dulcius ambrosia– (96)
a kiss sweeter than sweet ambrosia

"Coda for Federico García Lorca" (113) is a homophonic imitation of
"Oda a Walt Whitman" by Federico García Lorca.

The first 26 copies of this book are lettered and signed.

This copy is letter_____

Made in the USA
Charleston, SC
20 April 2010